Chasing Rainbows: Reflections on Infertility & Motherhood

Robyn Flynn

BookLeaf Publishing

India | USA | UK

Chasing Rainbows: Reflections on Infertility
& Motherhood © 2023 Robyn Flynn

All rights reserved.

No part of this publication may be
reproduced, stored in a retrieval system, or
transmitted, in any form or by any means,
electronic, mechanical, photocopying,
recording or otherwise, without the prior
written permission of the presenters.

Robyn Flynn asserts the moral right to be
identified as author of this work.

Presentation by *BookLeaf Publishing*

Web: www.bookleafpub.com

E-mail: info@bookleafpub.com

ISBN:9789358319149

First edition 2023

DEDICATION

For Peyton

Wanting

Late at night,
I found myself wanting.
Wanting to know you.
Wanting to see you.
Wanting to breathe you in.

What is that feeling?
That hole in my heart,
Waiting to be filled.

This wanting did not yet have a name but I could
smell it, picture it, feel it.
Your soft skin, your golden hair, your blue eyes.

I wanted you before I knew you.
I knew you before I wanted you.

Negative

Each month, the test is negative.
Always.
I've come to expect it.
Predict it.
Know it.
And yet…

I allow myself to hope.

Maybe.
Maybe.
Maybe.

The seconds on the timer tick down.

Maybe.
Maybe.
Maybe.

The alarms sounds.

Maybe.
Maybe.
Maybe.

Deep breath.

Maybe.
Maybe.
Maybe.

Glance.

Negative.

I knew it.

Trying

"At least it's fun to try!" they say.

Fun to try. Sure.

I can't remember the last time the trying was fun.

Circled dates on the calendar.

Peeing on sticks and in cups.

Legs in the air.

Logging.

Tracking.

Trying.

So methodical and clinical and scientific.

I smile.

"Yup. It's fun to try."

Too Fat

"You're too fat to be a mother."

The doctor's words cut like a knife, tearing through my flesh and piercing my heart.

I wince.

My fault.

This is all my fault.

Too fat?

Maybe I am.

This misery is mine.

I created this.

This dark storm cloud that hangs over our house isn't going away.

You deserve this.

This is your punishment.

This is what you've wrought.

Just lose the weight.

Then, you'll be deserving.

Deserving of love.

Deserving of respect.

Deserving of compassion.

Deserving of care.

Deserving of motherhood.

Shelley

"Put down your phone, your brain will turn to
mush."

"Why do you spend so much time on that
thing?"

"Don't air your dirty laundry for the world to
see."

"How can you be so vulnerable?"

One woman.
One story.
One city.

She saw my pain.
She took the time.
She made a difference.

Shelley.
My angel.
My saving grace.
Bless you.

Mad Scientist

Vial, syringe.
Needle and swab.
I'm like a mad scientist,
This is my new job.

Mix medications,
One, two, three, four.
Find the right dose,
Open the right door.

Store cool and tight,
Keep light away,
Keep stabbing yourself,
Keep demons at bay.

Mixing and matching,
And prepping my stims.
Keeping stabbing your self,
Until the light dims.

Battered & Bruises

My belly is covered.
Covered with bruises.
Blue and purple and gold.
Play connect the spots.
Play connect the dots.
Holes so tiny, I feel like a sieve.
Each hole evidence of my failure.
My hope is starting to drain.
Are the holes in my belly to blame?
I wince with each prick.
The needles are sharp.
So sharp.
I wince.
Not because of the needle.
But the voice inside me.
She gets louder every day.
"You'll never be a mother."
I wince.

BFP

Negative.
It's always negative.
But I take the test just the same.

Maybe.
Maybe.
Maybe.

I wait. I bargain. I plead.

Maybe.
Maybe.
Maybe.

Wait.
Wait.
Wait.

Two pink lines where there's usually one?!
My heart starts to race.

Life. Your life.
It begins now.

I wanted you.

I knew you.
I made you.

Daddy

"Make me a daddy."

Your sweet request echoes in my heart.

The years of trying.

The letdowns.

The heart ache.

Our angel in the sky.

It all led us here.

To this moment.

To this life.

We created a life.

Together.

Our love.

Our magic.

Our belief.

We did this.

It finally worked.

You're going to be a daddy.

Life

Barely the size of a sweet pea,
Nestled deep inside my womb.
I feel you.

Who will you be?
What will you become?
I feel you.

Tiny fingers, hands and feet.
You're growing every day.
I feel you.

Where will we go?
How will we do?
I feel you.

This magical moment is ours for the taking.
We are united as one.
I feel you.

Motherhood

Motherhood doesn't happen in an instant.

It's a slow, winding road.

It's sleepovers with your nephew, and movies
with your niece.

It's playtime with siblings and cousins so small.

It's experience after experience, each building
like blocks.

It builds and builds.

Until there are two lines.

And every single moment of your life has
brought you to this moment.

You are here.
I feel you.

Time

Time begins to lose all meaning.

The stratosphere cracks open, devouring us whole.

We remain one. Safe. Nestled.

Life is flipped on its axis.

Drip. Drip. Drip.

You're coming, they say.

But you're already here.

I feel you.

Here

A cold, sterile room
A hanging blue sheet.
I'm shaking so hard,
It's time we should meet.

Beeping machines,
And voices go by.
It's time, little one.
It's time to say hi.

My belly is numb,
I can't see anymore.
Daddy is here.
Mommy is sore.

43 hours
Of waiting for you
It's time, little one.
You know what to do.

Knife to flesh.
Flesh to heart.
My body is numb.
I've been ripped apart.

Take a deep breath,
And let out a yelp.
You're here, little one.
Thanks to the doctor's help.

Torn in two,
So you can be free.
We're no longer one,
Now, we are three.

Skin to Skin

I can't believe you're here.

Your skin is on mine.
Your eyes, so blue.
Your hair, so golden.

I wanted you before I knew you.
I knew you before I wanted you.

And now you are here.

Love So Big

I'd always heard
That it's a love so big
You can't possibly understand
Until it happens.
Until they're here.
Until you meet them.
A love so big
You'd do anything for them.
A love so big
That those late night feedings
Don't bother you so much.
A love so big
That you become different.
A different person.
A different soul.
A love so big
That there's meaning.
Meaning to this life.
Meaning to this world.
Meaning to MY life.
A love so big.
You are my love.
A love so big.

Tiny Cries

When you picture a newborn,
You picture screaming, crying, wailing.
Poop. Puke. Cracked nipples.
Everyone says it's miserable.
Hard.
So hard.
The hardest thing you'll ever do.
But I have found nothing but peace.
Calm. Serenity. Joy.
Your cries are soft,
As if to gently rouse me from sleeping into
waking.
As if to let me know you're awake.
No screaming, no crying, no wailing.
There's no need.
A gentle whimper.
Tiny cries in the dark.
"Mommy, I'm awake. I'm hungry."
You know I'll come.
You know I'll be there.
I'll always be there for you, little one.

Pure Magic

Everyone keeps checking in.
"How are you holding up?"
"How are you doing?"
"How are you coping?"
I keep hearing how hard this is supposed to be.
I'm supposed to be exhausted.
I'm supposed to be frazzled.
I'm supposed to be miserable.
But I'm not?
I slip into motherhood like a pair of sweats.
With ease. Happiness. Comfort.
I can't help but feel
Like I was meant for this life.
Like I was meant to be a mom.
Your mom.
I know what to do.
I know what you need.
Daddy thinks it's magic when I know just what
to do.
But your blood is my blood.
It courses through me veins.
Daddy is right, you know.
Being your mom is magic.
Magic.
Pure magic.

Giggly Girl

The happiest girl.
The most joyful baby.
Our giggly girl.
Your smile lights up the room
And our hearts.
A tiny princess.
The sweetest of hearts.
You've captured that magic.
Spread your joy, baby girl.
Share it with the world.

Sweet Potato

Tiny babies resemble potatoes.
"She's such a potato."
An off-hand comment that would become so
much.
Our tiny potato.
Our sweetest potato.
A nickname we never intended to give you.
A nickname I'm sure you'll despise down the
line.
But for now,
You're our sweet potato.
The littlest potato.

A Love Like Ours

Your daddy and I love to be silly.
We laugh and dance and play.
Couples don't do enough of that.
Play, I mean.
There's magic there.
There's joy.
This family unit is everything.
We love so hard, and laugh even harder.
You're the brightest spot in all of our days.
You complete us.
I thought that nothing could compete
With the love your daddy and I shared.
But the love the three of us share?
This love is something special.
No one will ever know
A love like ours.

Who Will You Be?

Who will you be, one day?
Will you follow your dreams,
And chase magic and love?
Will your ambition drive you
To do incredible things?
Will your heart find stillness
And seek out a quiet life?
A life filled with love.
Purpose.
Meaning.
Stillness.
Will you change the world, baby girl?
Will you do incredible things?
Who will you be?
What will be in your heart?
My wish for you is to be kind.
To be kind to others,
But also to yourself.
To treat yourself with the utmost respect.
Love. Love yourself and everything there.
You are the most special girl.
The most beautiful girl.
The funniest, silliest, most playful girl.
Don't lose that sense of wonder.
Don't lose that sense of joy and play.

Who will you be, baby girl?
Will you dare to dream? Dare to be great?
Will you listen to your heart and follow your
dreams?
Who will you be?
I hope that you will choose kindness.
Find magic wherever you go.
Who will you be?
Will you be brave?
I hope you travel by yourself.
Find new and exciting worlds.
Depend on you.
Trust yourself.
Go to the movies alone.
Find joy in solitude.
Make shadow puppets in the dark.
Laugh often.
Love big.
Who will you be, baby girl?
Find your people.
The kind of people that put your heart and mind
at ease.
People who, when you meet them, feel like like
they've known you for years.
Trust that feeling.
Seek it out.
Refuse to settle for less than great.
Who will you be, baby girl?
I can't wait to see.